Reflections on the Beatitudes

DATE DUE

CHURCH OF SCOTLAND GENERAL ASSEMBLY
— 2001 —

Reflections on the Beatitudes

Reflections on the Beatitudes at the
General Assembly of the Church of Scotland in 2001

THE RIGHT REVEREND JOHN MILLER

'You are the light of the world'

SAINT ANDREW PRESS

First published in 2002 by
SAINT ANDREW PRESS
121 George Street
Edinburgh EH2 4YN

Reprinted 2002

ISBN 0 7152 0802 0

British Library Cataloguing in Publication Data
A catalogue record for this book is available from the British Library

This book has been published with grant assistance from the
Drummond Trust, 3 Pitt Terrace, Stirling

Printed and bound in the United Kingdom by Mackay & Inglis Limited, Glasgow

Contents

Saturday Evening Reflection

And seeing the crowds, Jesus went up into the mountain …

(Matthew 5:1–12)

These verses from Matthew's Gospel constitute one of the best-known of all Christian texts, one of the most influential pieces of literature in history. From what is called 'the Sermon on the Mount', this part is often called 'the Beatitudes'. Tomorrow, and in the times of worship which open the successive sessions of this Assembly, I shall be inviting you to think of the people highlighted in the Beatitudes, the people whom Jesus lists among 'the Blessed'.

But tonight we begin with the opening words. The opening sentence is this: *And seeing the crowds, Jesus went up into the mountain*. To my mind, these words describe our own situation: here are people, gathered around Jesus, listening to what he says, waiting to hear where he is going to lead us. That's us, in our General Assembly.

One of the persistent problems for scholars is to try to work out whether Jesus taught the whole crowd, or

1

just his disciples. Did he go up the mountainside so that his voice might carry to the whole assembled multitude? Or did he, rather, go away from the noise of the crowd to talk intimately with his disciples? On balance, the scholars consider that Jesus was explaining the Hebrew Scriptures in a new way for his own followers, his own disciples, while the crowd were near, within hearing distance.

In exact terms, this sets out our own very situation. We count ourselves as disciples of the Lord. Our business has already begun. This morning, we started the proceedings. This afternoon, our meeting was celebrated in the time-honoured Lord High Commissioner's Garden Party. Those of us with tickets – large numbers of us – went in through the gate, watched by crowds of spectators. We were aware of the multitude, the crowds.

While we could hardly say that the eyes of the world are upon us, certainly many people know that the General Assembly is meeting this week. The newspapers, the media, know. The communities from which we have all come – they know. The tourists and bystanders from this afternoon, they know. Perhaps others, too, know. We are aware of the great world out there, the world which will be the subject of many of our debates here in the Assembly, the world which we believe God made and for which we believe Christ died.

But, for this week, we have come away from the world. We have come away, as it were, to the mountainside, gathering to hear what the Lord has to say to us. We are here awaiting the teaching, expecting the teaching, dependent upon the teaching of the Lord.

This is, surely, the very attitude which we should be adopting as the General Assembly proceeds. We anticipate that the Lord will be speaking to us, teaching us, guiding us. We shall be relying on the work undertaken by so many hundreds of people throughout the past year, as the Reports are presented, the discussion pursued, the decisions taken and recorded. But, behind the work of everyone, we are seeking to discern what the Lord is wanting us to hear. What teaching has he for us?

That's what we're here for. Tonight, as much as ever. This verse again:

> And seeing the crowds, Jesus went up into the mountain. And when he was set, his disciples came to him. And he opened his mouth and taught them.

Sunday Morning Sermon
St Giles Cathedral

You are the salt of the earth, said Jesus.
You are the light of the world, he said.

Jesus addressed these words to the people who had gathered round him on the side of the mountain. Here is one of the features of what has come to be known as the Sermon on the Mount: throughout that sermon, Jesus states the most astounding things in the most simple, matter-of-fact manner. We know less about the people who surrounded him on the mountainside than we do about one another here. As you look about you this morning, you will perhaps see people you know well. There will be others whom you recognise, some who are completely unknown to you. But as for the people to whom Jesus addressed his words that day, we know nothing about most, and tantalisingly little about any. Yet he said to them: 'You are the salt of the earth; you are the light of the world'.

We have no reason to think that they were other than the ordinary people who had heard him before, but who had found his words the words of eternal life. From that company who heard Jesus that day, we do

4

know something of Peter, of James, of John, of Mary, of Thomas, and later of Paul, Barnabas, Dorcas, Silas and a few others. But they, and all the other men and women whose names are known now only to God, all of them received that affirmation and that call. The flavour of their faith, the brightness of their witness, arose from what they had learned from Jesus. Nowhere more than here in the Sermon on the Mount.

And so it is for us today. Ordinary people, listening for the Words of eternal life. 'You are the salt of the earth. Yes. You. You are the light of the world. Yes, you.'

The church faces huge difficulties today. There are a great many signs that the old order is changing. Perhaps this has not been your experience of the church, but it has been that of others. There are many who carry responsibility for keeping the church going through these times, and for them the burden has become extremely heavy. Whether as office-bearers, fewer and older, having to do more and more duties in order to sustain local church life; whether as administrators, adapting to rapid change with an increasing number of difficult decisions; whether as church members, witnessing the autumn and winter of a church life which once nourished and sustained them; or whether as ministers of the Gospel, and full-time lay servants of the church, who have understood themselves as called by the Lord to serve his church and to feed his sheep, but are faced now with an overwhelming secularisation even of the church itself. It seems that the patterns which our grandparents and great-grandparents established will not serve the present day.

Small wonder that to many people the prospect for the church seems dark. Some are full of despair, and have lost hope. They hear the truth in the words of John Milton, in his poem *Samson Agonistes*. Samson, blinded by his Philistine captors, says in his despair:

> *Dark, dark, dark, irrecoverably dark.*
> *Total eclipse, without all hope of day.*

Yes, some people fear that that is the prospect for the church.

But the prophets of our ancestors in faith the Jews, the glorious prophets of Israel – they understood God's mind on such matters. They make it clear that in times of trouble we must seek God's will. And it may not be comfortable. Indeed, the prophet Amos asks his hearers (5:18–20):

> *Why would you have the day of the LORD?*
> *It is darkness and not light;*
> *Is not the day of the LORD darkness and not light,*
> *And gloom with no brightness in it?*

In today's reading, Isaiah speaks of what the Lord requires. Even the most intense religious devotion is irrelevant: fasting, sackcloth and ashes, and bowing of the head count for nothing. The Lord calls for nothing less than feeding the hungry, welcoming the poor into our homes, and clothing those who have no clothes.

But now we must frame the question: what is being asked of us in this difficult time? What is the Lord asking of us? And, as so often, we shall find that the Lord shows us the answer in those who count for little or nothing in this world's eyes.

From thirty years in a housing-scheme parish, I have observed this. The congregation to which I went thirty years ago had begun life in a breathtakingly beautiful building, set in the midst of a mature woodland. Walls of plate glass encouraged worshippers to include in their thoughts about God both the glory of nature and the teeming life of the city. But the glass suffered from flying stones, the windows had to be bricked up, and the family of faith became preoccupied with the state of the building. Absolutely everything that took place had to raise money for the bills. Even the children's parties at Christmas had to make a profit. Not only that, but anxiety about the building meant that the congregation viewed the surrounding community as hostile, and if any young ones set foot in the grounds they were chased away with shouts. The smashing of the final window, twice in a week, and my fear about how the congregation were going to react, suddenly revealed to me that the energy of the faithful was being diverted from its true purpose: we had come to care more about the building than about the people it was supposedly there to serve. We had allowed the structures to take precedence over everything else. But structures, whether buildings or systems or patterns or organisations – structures are secondary. The Gospel comes first.

Our confrontation with this apparent disaster in our buildings forced us to reflect on what we were really there for. We held meetings of the whole congregation, and in discussion and Bible study we looked at our plight. We saw that the church's business is nothing less than the Word of Life. The Church is not a building. Nor is the church merely a social agency, providing care and help to the needy. Far less is it a stern parent, seeking to direct the behaviour of old and young according to a strict set of rules.

The church is the community of faith, listening to the Lord, listening for the Word of Life, the unchanging Lord. *Jesus Christ is the same yesterday and today and for ever* (Hebrews 13:8). To be witnesses to this truth is the whole purpose of the church. In a time of change, we often try to hold on to the received patterns, the buildings, the organisations, the structures which served an earlier day. But everything can go, except the Gospel. As a church, the Word of Life is our reason for existence.

In the local congregation, once we had faced the way in which our focus on the buildings was distorting our life of faith, we made some decisions. The buildings could survive only by the generosity of others and by the grace of God. And they might not survive. But we could serve them no longer. They must now serve the Gospel. We swallowed our pride and applied for grants. Some were given, and we began to open the buildings up. There was a nearly-new sale, a midnight café all through the night at weekends, and the Bible study group had a central role.

Having decided not to worry constantly about money, people began to enjoy their church life. More and more, they took part in community life with their neighbours, in tenants' groups, health groups, pensioners' action, children's work, school boards, youth work. Even the services of worship had more life, more noise, deeper silence. What had begun as a crisis became a point of new growth. The Gospel, not the building, was now nearer the heart of the church.

The truth of all this is understood most surely of all by a company of people whose character has been known for 2,000 years. I speak of those who are the subjects of the Beatitudes. Enumerated at the beginning of the Sermon on the Mount, they are the ones who know God's secrets. But the world, which values only success and power, simply does not notice them. The list begins: *Blessed are the poor in spirit, for theirs is the Kingdom of Heaven.*

'*The poor in spirit.*' It was from a Franciscan, Albert Gelin, that I learned this interpretation: '*Blessed are those who have the spirit of the poor*'. The poor are like this: they have no resources outside themselves. They have no wealth to spend, no property to sell, no bought house, nothing set aside 'for a rainy day'. They search down the sides of chairs for pennies for the children's bus fares. They have no slippers or dressing-gown if they are taken into hospital, no money to buy birthday presents or Christmas presents unless they go into debt. If they come into money, they know what friendship means, and they will often give all they have to others. The poor often think of God, because there is no other help.

And *the spirit of the poor* is found in others, others whose material circumstances may be quite different. All kinds of events can bring us face to face with our fragility, our mortality, our utter dependence on the One who has given us Life. Tragedy can do this – the death of a dear one, old or young. Sudden illness can do it – catastrophe or disappointment, the approach of old age, fear of death, compassion for the distressed. Such human events and occurrences can engender the spirit of a poor person in the heart and life of someone with great possessions. When thus challenged by life, they will often see that their possessions are not theirs at all, and instead they will use them for others. And Jesus affirms that those who have the spirit of the poor keep company with God.

The others on that list are known to you – the others who keep company with God. Those who mourn; the meek; those who long for what is right; the merciful, the pure in heart, the peacemakers, those who suffer for doing what is right. All these know what really matters in life. They know, above all, that structures are secondary; that the Word of Life is found in the Gospel of Jesus Christ. On this path, the church and each one will find life.

So there we are. We know the problems full well. And the Gospel's guidance is before us. Are we ready to follow?

And our hope lies not in some formula, not in any plan. Our hope lies in a person, in him whose life is our example, whose words are eternal life. He is the one who has borne our griefs and carried our sorrows, and he will be all in all for us. And he it is who says:

> *You are the salt of the earth;*
> *You are the light of the world.*

It is an affirmation – and a challenge. Jesus says it to the church, and he says it to you.

Sunday Evening Reflection

> Blessed are the meek, for they shall inherit the earth.
>
> (Matthew 5:33–48)

The opening worship sets the context for everything we do at the General Assembly. At this Assembly, I have chosen the readings from the Sermon on the Mount, this central Christian text. And at each of these times of worship, we shall look at what are known as 'the Beatitudes' – Jesus' statements about people who can truly be counted as keeping company with God; people who can be counted as having such a state of blessedness that they could really be called 'happy'.

This morning, I looked at those who have the spirit of the poor. Tonight, *Blessed are the meek*.

You've maybe heard the little joke about this beatitude, about the meek inheriting the earth. It goes: 'Blessed are the meek, for they shall inherit the earth, if that's all right with you'! It's not offered as a compliment, if you call someone 'meek' nowadays. It's usually a criticism of their unwillingness to stand up for themselves. This is a hard world, competitive, and it will search out your weaknesses. Poor show if you can't speak up for your interests. This is no time to be meek. Our culture would say: 'The meek may inherit the next world, but they'll not get far in this one'.

So what is it, to be meek? There's something of it in this little illustration. Years ago, a good friend of mine was unemployed. He had had a very well-paid job as an executive. Now he had to go and sign on. He told me that, on his first day signing on, he was standing in the queue. The queue seemed to be taking for ever. My friend, quite tall, was sighing and tutting, and looking impatiently about, and hopping from foot to foot. The man behind him in the queue tapped him gently on the elbow and said: 'Steady on, son. You haven't got the patience of the working class!' Being meek means putting up with things patiently, not constantly forcing the issue, not irritably demanding your required response.

Does the word as we use it today mean what it meant in the time when Jesus spoke to the disciples in his Sermon on the Mount? Yes. If we look at it, I think we'll see it means the same. It's the word used by Paul, when he speaks of Jesus as putting up with us (2 Corinthians 10:1) in his meekness and gentleness. It is the word used by Jesus of himself on Palm Sunday, when he quotes Zechariah: 'Your king is coming to you, meek and riding on a donkey'. It is the word Jesus uses of himself when he calls those who labour and are heavily laden. 'Take my yoke upon you and learn of me, for I am meek and lowly in heart: and you will find rest for your souls'. It is this characteristic of patience, not forcing the issue, accepting what happens, tolerating other people's self-advancement.

And what does Jesus say of those people whom the world, as it rushes along, leaves behind? Does he say: 'They'll get their reward in heaven'? No: 'they shall inherit the earth'.

It is a promise.

Jesus looks at those whose character is patient, tolerant, unassuming, modest; he looks at the meek, and contradicts the wisdom of the world. He says: 'The meek shall inherit the earth'.

It is embodied for us in Jesus himself. For Jesus submitted meekly to the indignity of arrest and trial; he accepted the injustice and the brutality of the illegal process. He did not create a stir, did not demand his rights; he was humble, he was obedient unto death, even death on the cross.

Jesus singled out the meek and included them in his list of the blessed. God understands their ways. Jesus did not say, as we might: 'they ought to inherit the earth'. No; 'they shall inherit the earth'. It's a statement. When the Lord's day comes, it will be.

Monday Morning Reflection

Blessed are they that mourn, for they shall be comforted.

(Matthew 6:1–14)

The communion service, on the Monday morning of each Assembly, forms a central role in the whole General Assembly. For we are given this wonderful opportunity to share in the unity of Christ through the simple gifts of bread and wine, a celebration of our membership of the family of faith.

The powerful reading from the Sermon on the Mount reminds us, however, that it is in the secret place of our heart that God meets us. And even as we meet publicly and visibly together, we recognise that God sees the heart. And it is against the background of that reading that we reflect now on another of the Beatitudes.

Each of the Beatitudes comes at you out of the blue, listing the people who count in the Kingdom of Heaven. And if any one statement was going to prove the oddity of the Beatitudes, this is it: *Blessed are they that mourn; for they shall be comforted.*

Who on earth would include, in the list of the blessed, people whose life was devastated by the loss of someone they loved?

Think of the characteristics of a person in mourning:

- Pre-occupied with the pain, the actual, bodily, physical pain of the person's absence.

- Isolated and unreachable.

- Powerless to alter the situation.

- Prone to anger at the course that life has taken.

- Locked and unable to move forward, trapped in grief like a ship in pack ice.

Blessed? Such a person as this, blessed? If you have known such a person, or if you have been such a person, you will know the devastation which mourning brings – how a carefree, joyful family life can be utterly changed; how a hopeful, creative path can become utterly dark.

But look again at these characteristics of a person in mourning. A person in grief is focused to an intense degree on the importance not of himself or herself, but of someone else. Perhaps for the first time, they have fathomed their own vulnerability, their own need of others. They have been confronted with the fragility of human life, and also with its value beyond price. Is any sorrow greater than that of a mother? You will remember those words from the prophet Jeremiah, found in Matthew's Gospel concerning the slaughter of the innocents in Bethlehem: 'A voice was heard in Ramah, wailing and loud lamentation, Rachel weeping for her children; she refused to be consoled, for they were no more'.

A person in mourning is faced with the unchangeable facts of death. They long for it not to be true. And even if there had to be death, they wish that they themselves could have taken the place of the one they loved. You will remember the grief-stricken words of King David on the death of his rebellious son: 'O Absalom, my son, my son Absalom! Would God I had died instead of you, O Absalom, my son, my son.' Here is David, like numberless others since then, wishing he had had the opportunity to lay down his life for the one he loved so much. Greater love has no one than this, said Jesus.

The close encounter with death changes people's perspective. A person in mourning knows now what is really important in life. It's not material goods, or worldly success; not pleasure, nor travel, nor power. To a person who mourns, even their own good health may seem a burden, a cause for guilt or regret. For they have learned that the important thing in life is the tie of love between one and another.

Jesus puts these people among the ones who understand the thoughts of God. He directs people's attention to them, and he calls them 'blessed'. And then he says: 'For they shall be comforted'.

Who is he to say this? These are not soft, empty words. This is not the wishful thinking of some purveyor of cheap consolation. This is the ultimate assurance, given by the Saviour of the World, that all things are in the hand of God. The man who says this is the man who in the company of his close disciples called Lazarus forth from the grave. This is the one who for our sakes faced the pains of death, and on the third day rose from the dead. And to all who mourn, as to his disciples after he had risen from the dead, he says: 'Peace be with you'.

Tuesday Morning Reflection

> Blessed are they that hunger and thirst after righteousness, for they shall be satisfied.
>
> (Matthew 6:16–24)

These beautiful verses direct our thoughts yet again to a set of values which are in contradiction to the expressed values of our society. They encourage in us a sense of the risks to which faith calls us: no treasures on earth for thieves and robbers to steal, but treasure in heaven, and there your heart will be also.

Today's Beatitude is this: *Blessed are those who hunger and thirst for righteousness, for they shall be satisfied.*

We are fortunate indeed that we seldom have to suffer hunger and thirst. Most of us have had a good breakfast this morning. Not so across more than half the world. Not so, either, in the Palestine of Jesus' day. Many people there would be no strangers to the physical pain of hunger. And in the words of this verse, Jesus confers his affirmation on those who hunger and thirst to see right being done.

There are people like that. In our generation, we have been privileged to witness the character of outstanding men and women whose courage in the face of brutal repression, courage even unto death, led to a new age in South Africa. That hunger for righteousness, that thirst to see right prevail, is epitomised in South Africa's former President Nelson Mandela. He, and others who lived through 'the struggle', lived to see the new age begin – they were to that extent satisfied in this life, although the new phases of the struggle confront them still.

But there are others who, in their own setting, hunger and thirst for righteousness without seeing right prevail: people such as the Dalai Lama of Tibet, Aung San Suu Kyi the human rights leader in Burma, and many others whose causes have not come to such public notice. There are heroic figures such as these upon the world stage.

But there are heroic figures nearer home. Some you will know yourself. I think of a retired school secretary, now in her eighties, who campaigned for half her life for justice in South Africa. I think of John, who stands up for people who are 'invisible-ised' by officials. At the Housing, the Benefits, or the Employment, John accompanies them, argues for them, makes people listen to them. If Sheriff's Officers are coming to carry out a warrant sale, John will gather friends to fill the house so full that the Sheriff's Officers can't get in. Such are the ordinary people who take up the cause of justice at great cost to themselves, risking their jobs, losing opportunities for promotion, becoming targets of criticism, hatred and violence from opponents, and objects of ridicule and scorn to uncomprehending friends.

Such people know that the struggle sometimes seems unavailing; but that makes no difference to them. They go on anyway. But it is the persistence which they demonstrate that Jesus singles out here, telling his disciples, telling the world, that the tenacity of such heroes will not be in vain. He says: 'They shall be satisfied'.

> *Blessed are they that hunger and thirst for righteousness, for they shall be satisfied.*

Wednesday Morning Reflection

Blessed are the merciful, for they shall obtain mercy.

(Matthew 6:25–34)

In unforgettable imagery, this reading draws for us a picture of the providence of God. Jesus speaks of God who feeds the birds of the air and who clothes with beauty the lilies of the field. Jesus makes the statement, simple and direct, that life is more than food or clothing or length of days. Life consists in seeking God's kingdom.

Against this background, I invite you this morning to reflect upon this Beatitude: *Blessed are the merciful, for they shall obtain mercy*. Once again, Jesus affirms a characteristic which seldom brings worldly success. Although the quality of mercy is praised in poem and novel, in the hard grind of daily life it does not often make an appearance. Sometimes, as in the admirable Jubilee 2000 campaign to eliminate the international debt of some of the world's poorest countries, mercy makes an appearance on the world stage. To show mercy often involves just that kind of sacrifice – a loss of personal rights, a readiness to relinquish one's right to just repayment, a generosity of spirit which will bring no reward.

In the parable, the Good Samaritan showed mercy to the man who had fallen among thieves. It was this rare practical goodness which the lawyer recognised as an irresistible sign of the right way to live.

And what of the church? Jesus saw mercy as of eternal value. And, expensive and unprofitable though it may be, mercy is surely a vital ingredient of the life of the true church. It is the counterbalance to law, the affirmation of a higher way.

I talked once to a woman who had suffered a lot in a hard, brutal marriage. She was a devout believer, and prayed to God to help her through. If her husband caught her at prayer, kneeling perhaps at her bedside, he would kick her terribly. She prayed that God would give her strength to love her husband still.

Eventually, for her own sake and for her children's, she left him and made a separate life for herself and the children. After some years, her husband suffered a severe stroke. She heard how ill he was, and she brought him home from hospital to her house. And there she looked after him. He was unable to move without assistance, scarcely able to talk. He was, literally, at her mercy.

She told me that she felt that all her earlier prayers had been answered, and that in spite of all that she had suffered at his hands she was able to love him still. Here had been the perfect opportunity for her to level the scores. She could easily have taken pleasure in the power that had come to her, she could quite understandably have exacted some form of recompense for all that she had had to go through. But instead she had found that she had been given the gift of love. She showed mercy.

And was it all for nothing? Jesus said: *Blessed are the merciful, for they shall obtain mercy*. Thank God for that. If we can show mercy, there'll be hope for us yet.

Thursday Morning Reflection

Blessed are the peacemakers, for they shall be called the children of God.

(Matthew 7:7–15)

We cannot fathom the peace of God. We cannot measure or weigh it. Paul the Apostle describes it in these very words: *'the peace of God which passes all understanding'* (Philippians 4:7). Such peace as this is not peace at any price, but peace which goes hand in hand with justice, making the world a better place. Jeremiah spoke of the harm done by false prophets, who proclaimed: 'Peace. Peace' when there was no peace.

But here, Jesus highlights the value of those who make peace. At the heart of all religions is the quest for peace. And in the church, we are always seeking to enter and to share in the peace of Christ.

I want to tell you of Andy. Growing up in a mining village, a community divided by religious differences, Andy was a battle-hardened Protestant. As a young man, he became a regular soldier and served in the Second World War. On a voyage through the Mediterranean, he was on a ship which was torpedoed and sunk. Many, even of the survivors, were lost when they were machine-gunned in the water by enemy planes. Andy was no swimmer, but he stayed afloat by clinging to wreckage. He could not have survived those twenty-four hours in the water, had it not been for another man who encouraged him and helped him. This companion was a Forces chaplain, a Roman Catholic priest. Andy's bitter prejudice could not survive this life-saving experience. He never forgot those long hours in the water and his companion the priest whose encouragement helped him to live.

In the years following his return to civilian life, Andy found many obstacles and difficulties in his way. But, in time, he emerged as a significant community leader, devoted to improving community life, to building bridges between old and young, and making peace between the long-divided religious communities of the West of Scotland.

On a Remembrance Sunday more than fifty years after the event, Andy told the church congregation about that wartime encounter between himself and his fellow-survivor in the perilous waters of the Mediterranean. A peace had been made then in Andy which goes on making peace today.

What greater or more worthy pursuit could we engage in than making peace, the activity which Jesus says marks people out as belonging to the family of God?

Blessed are the peacemakers, for they shall be called the children of God.

Friday Morning Reflection

Blessed are the pure in heart, for they shall see God.

(Matthew 7:1–6)

Today's reading from the Sermon on the Mount is as relevant to us today as it was to those who had gathered to hear Jesus on that hillside. For most of us are brilliantly clear-sighted about the faults of others, while we are blind to far greater faults in ourselves. We can detect a speck in the eye of another, yet do not notice the plank of wood sticking out of our own. It is against that backdrop that we consider today the words of Jesus, *Blessed are the pure in heart, for they shall see God.*

The pure in heart have perfect sight. Not for them a focus on the faults of others. Not for them some competitive assessment of their own virtues compared with the sins of their neighbour.

As for the church – pure in heart? Often, even the churches compete with one another, one congregation and another, one denomination and another, looking for faults in the other when faults greater still are to be found at home.

But you have met the pure in heart, I'm sure, as I too have had the privilege of meeting them in my own life. What is it that marks them out? What characterises the pure in heart? Like people who can find white heather on the wide, purple-covered hillside, the eyes of the pure in heart are attuned to seeing goodness. It is always goodness which attracts their eye. In a throng of problems, they unerringly pick out the point of growth, the place from which some good will come. They are not willing to spend time on idle words. We know people like this. Some are young, some are old. Some are well, some infirm. They have in common the ability to draw strength from an unfailing hope.

I think of Agnes, whose life was never easy, who has carried many sorrows. Now in her eighties, she still loves to dance. Her favourite word is 'lovely'. 'Lovely', she'll say when someone speaks approvingly to her. 'Lovely', she'll say when she hears of some good thing. She won't listen to gossip; it's of no interest to her. She won't hear a word against anyone; she says there's always some explanation that we don't know. She's always thankful for a new day.

So is it simply a gift, being 'pure in heart'? Sometimes it seems so, for it is found in unexpected and utterly unpredictable circumstances. Yet surely it is a gift which we can acquire, an attribute which we can develop. It is possible, by vigilance and by prayer and by the grace of God, to simplify and purify the focus of our life. And the reward is beyond price. For Jesus says:

Blessed are the pure in heart, for they shall see God.

Friday Evening Reflection

Blessed are those who are persecuted for righteousness' sake, for theirs is the kingdom of heaven.

(Matthew 7.15–29)

Tonight brings us to the final Beatitude. *Blessed are those who are persecuted for righteousness' sake, for theirs is the kingdom of heaven.* Once again, Jesus singles out a style of life, a pattern of existence, which brings people into God's company. But who would want to be among them?

You see it all the time. The person who points out malpractice in the workplace. The consultant surgeon who sees incompetence being covered up. The civil servant who recognises a case of collusion or corruption. If someone in those circumstances brings the matter to public attention, they become what is sometimes called a whistle-blower. And even if what they have drawn attention to has been calling out to be exposed, often the messengers themselves are regarded as the troublemakers. They lose their friends, they forfeit the alliance with their colleagues, they can lose their job. But did they do anything wrong? Did they not simply stand up for what is right? But, in the world's terms, they will often be the loser.

They are picked on, victimised, unjustly criticised. For such as these, Jesus predicts exactly the same as he had done in the earlier verse for those who have the spirit of the poor. *The kingdom of heaven is theirs*. And how like the poor these persecuted individuals are. They too are confronted with huge, undeserved difficulties. They too are understood only by others who have been through the same thing. But for these, as for those with the spirit of the poor, their experience has opened them to the hope which faith offers. They become companions of God.

But in this final Beatitude, Jesus adds something more. For here, as he speaks to his disciples, he doesn't simply say: 'Blessed are these, for they shall receive this reward'. No. This time, alone of the Beatitudes, he points it directly at the disciples. *Blessed are you*, he said, *when people revile you and persecute you and utter all kinds of evil against you falsely for my sake*. Even here, at the very beginning of his active life of service, Jesus was aware of the forces of the world which were already planning his death. He warned his followers of what they would face.

Not us; not in our day; not here in Scotland. But among our visitors from overseas this week have been men and women who have already suffered just as Jesus said, who have been reviled, persecuted and falsely accused for Jesus' sake. And inspired by our Lord's words, we are humbly able to say to them: 'Rejoice. Great is your reward in heaven, for that is the way they persecuted the prophets before you.' Truly, their names are written in heaven.

This has been the last of the eight Beatitudes, which form the introduction to the Sermon on the Mount. Jesus has set before his disciples this roll of honour, this series of people who count for nothing by the world's standard, but who in truth understand God better than anyone else in the world.

Two thousand years have borne out the truth with which Jesus brings the Sermon on the Mount to an end. Everyone who hears his words and acts on them will be like the man who built his house on a rock. No matter the storms, the house did not fall, because it had been founded upon a rock.

Closing Address

I shall not speak for long. I have spoken a lot over the past week. I do want to speak of the Assembly, of which this is the final part.

When one becomes Moderator, there is no way of knowing, until one steps onto this podium, whether or not one will actually manage to do what is required. So it was a great relief to me to discover that I did not freeze, or faint, or run for cover. Indeed, I sure you will have sensed that I enjoyed very much the communication between yourselves and the chair, which helped to shape the pattern of the debates. And I have been extremely grateful for the expressions of good wishes and for the assurances of the prayers of many people. These have been of great benefit and comfort to me, each one a support when the fragile edifice of one's confidence might have seemed likely to crumble. Thank you.

Prior to this Assembly, my last visit to the Usher Hall had been in 1965. I brought my then girlfriend, my teenaged girlfriend – yes, we later married – I brought her to a concert given by Simon and Garfunkel. We were away up there in the gods. (You can see I knew how to impress a girl.) The two singers were virtually unknown, and the hall was much less than half-full. Indeed, Paul Simon called us from the cheap seats to come down and take our place in the empty front stalls. Their song of the moment was *The Sound of Silence*.

Not much silence in the Usher Hall during the past week, as one by one the Reports came before us. No. Not much silence, but a great deal of listening. You Commissioners have worked extremely hard during the week. You have listened to the account of faithful, painstaking, unremitting work done by Boards and Committees over the past year, and you have been taking in the vision of the new landscape as it has been being outlined for us.

But you have not been engaged in a mere planning exercise. This General Assembly has been a spiritual event. In the worship at the beginning of each session of the Assembly, I wanted to direct attention to the Beatitudes, that unparalleled list of the people who know the thoughts of God. The spiritual Hall of Fame. In that litany of the Blessed are the qualities which give access to the Kingdom of Heaven:

> Those who have the spirit of the poor.
> Those who mourn.
> The meek.
> Those who hunger and thirst for righteousness.
> The merciful.
> The pure in heart.
> The peacemakers.
> Those who are persecuted for righteousness' sake.

It seemed to me that, with these qualities as our focus, we would have some perspective from which to look at the plans and decisions of the week. For a church which is looking to review and reform itself must constantly be relying on the guidance which God offers, and the words of Jesus illuminated by the Holy Spirit will prove to be our safeguard.

At the outset of the week, it seemed clear that huge questions were going to be raised. So it proved. It also seemed, from the Reports which were to come before us, that the major issues would be Priorities and Resourcing. That is, what are the Church of Scotland's priorities? How are these priorities going to be resourced, in terms of money and personnel?

To read the graphs and tables of church membership, baptisms, church weddings, new communicants, ministers, students in training for the ministry, is to be confronted with incontrovertible evidence from so many numerical measures that the church is getting smaller. But even if that be so, on Saturday evening, in his memorable 'Thank God for Money' speech, we heard from Leon Marshall, the retiring Convener of Stewardship and Finance, that the church's givings went up last year by 6.1 per cent, per capita giving by 6.8 per cent. The picture therefore is not by any means one of despair.

There is no doubt that both before the Assembly and during it, the Report on the Special Commission on Review and Reform – what came to be called the Neilson Commission – was recognised as inviting momentous change. And although perhaps the debate did not always reach the heights for which we had been preparing ourselves, the Assembly embraced its bold outlook. And a number of other major Reports provided the beginning of machinery to bring about elements of change.

Even the press seemed to detect a change of atmosphere in the church, recognising a new determination in the church to grapple with the realities of Scotland's current life and culture. It may be that the presence in today's Scotland of the Scottish Parliament has brought about a new awareness of the role of the church. Perhaps it is now more obvious that politics alone does not provide the answers to society's questions, and that the solutions benefit from acknowledging a spiritual dimension also. The Parliament itself has recognised the limitations of its own sphere, and has established communications with other elements of society, including most distinctly the churches of Scotland.

But on a number of occasions during this week, Commissioners have said: 'Ah, yes, but we've been here before'. 'There was the Anderson Report', people say. 'Then there was the Committee of Forty. Both of them said the same thing about where the church should be going, but nothing ever happened.' So we've been here before, and nothing has come of it.

But now we are here again. And what is going to make it different this time? What will make sure that this new vision doesn't drift away, doesn't become bogged down, impeded, hampered, hindered, obstructed, retarded, prevented? What will make sure that this time it is different? The answer to that is YOU.

For you will be going from here back to where you live and work. And that is where the Gospel comes to life. It is in the local setting that the family of faith takes root; it is there, in a parish, in the setting of a chaplaincy, in a workplace, that the life of faith flourishes. That is where you are going to be when this Assembly is only a memory.

It is in that local setting that the church will be renewed. And it will be renewed. Where you love your neighbour as you love yourself, the church will be renewed. For Christ is at home where love dwells.

Every Assembly is extraordinary. Certainly this has been an extraordinary Assembly. You have shared in a huge range of moods and a wide variety of emotions. There has been much laughter and there have been many tears. But you have also shared in making decisions which have the potential to give birth to the next generation of church life. John Cairns was quoted as saying in last Sunday's press: 'I can't tell you what the church would look like if these reforms were introduced'. That's true. We cannot see clearly what the shape of the church of the future is going to be. But among others the Neilson Report, the Presbytery Boundaries Report and the Ministry Report contain within them thinking which may liberate the Church of Scotland to develop the kind of patterns which will be capable of carrying the wonderful power of the Gospel to the world.

Some might say: 'This Assembly may have passed these Reports, but it doesn't represent what the church at large thinks'. I've heard those words on someone's lips. But this Assembly has passed them, and their possibilities are in your hands.

Perhaps you will think: 'But I go back to my congregation, to my presbytery, to my sphere of work, and there won't be another soul who was here, or who will understand what's needing to be done'. Perhaps you will think: 'I'm all on my own, and there's nothing I can do'.

Let me remind you of a story you know well, the story of Elijah, the most courageous of prophets. Locked in conflict with the king, he was afraid, and he fled for his life. He wished he were dead, and he prayed to the Lord to take his life away. Instead, the Lord directed him to the top of Mount Sinai. There the Lord sent a furious wind, but the Lord was not in the wind. Then the Lord sent an earthquake, but the Lord was not in the earthquake; then a fire, but the Lord was not in the fire. And after the fire, there was the soft whisper of a voice. And when Elijah heard it, he covered his face with his cloak. There the voice of the Lord assured Elijah that he was not alone, but that in Israel there were still 7,000 people, loyal to the Lord, of whom Elijah did not know. Remember Elijah when you go home to your parish, your presbytery, your sphere of life.

And let me tell you also of a woman of whom many of you have heard. Mary Slessor was a hard-workingmill girl and an unorthodox Sunday-school teacher in Dundee over 100 years ago. Inspired by David Livingstone, she became a missionary herself to tribes around Calabar in Nigeria. She inspired the people among whom she lived there, and she offered much-needed care. She brought an end to barbaric tribal customs, and she adopted over fifty African children who would otherwise have been left to die. In her well-thumbed Bible, still preserved in Dundee, above a passage referring to God's secure protection, she has boldly written: 'God and one, are always a majority'. When she died after a life of almost incredible practical effect in that area of Nigeria, a colleague said of her: 'Mary Slessor was a whirlwind and an earthquake, a fire and a still small voice, all in one'. Remember Mary Slessor when you go home.

And finally, let me remind you of the words of Jesus from the Sermon on the Mount, words so familiar to you that now perhaps you can hardly hear them. Yet they are the words of the ultimate affirmation and of the ultimate challenge:

> *You are the salt of the earth.*
> *You are the light of the world.*

Yes. You. *You are the light of the world.*

Go forth … and shine.